Diary of a Drummer Boy

Marlene Targ Brill

Illustrations by Michael Garland

The Millbrook Press
Brookfield, Connecticut

Acknowledgments

Beverly Millard, research librarian, Waukegan Historical Society
Terry Winschel, historian, Vicksburg National Military Park
Steven Bean, archivist, American Dental Association
Dee Jay Davis, Congressman Porter's Waukegan District Office
Diana Dretsky, historian, Lake County Museum
Bill Scarratt, Streatorland Historical Society
Dr. John Sellars, Library of Congress
Stuart Butler, National Archives
S. Michael Williams, Congressional Medal of Honor Society
Chad Wall, Nebraska State Historical Society
Jenny Epstein, WTTW Chicago, *Eleven* Magazine

Published by The Millbrook Press, Inc.
2 Old New Milford Road, Brookfield, Connecticut 06804

Text copyright © 1998 by Marlene Targ Brill
Illustrations copyright © 1998 by Michael Garland

Library of Congress Cataloging-in-Publication Data
Brill, Marlene Targ.
Diary of a drummer boy / Marlene Targ Brill; illustrations by Michael Garland.
p.   cm.
Includes bibliographical references (p.   -.)
Summary: The fictionalized diary of a twelve-year-old boy who joins the Union army
as a drummer, and ends up fighting in the Civil War.
ISBN 0-7613-0118-6 (lib. bdg.)
1. United States—History—Civil War, 1861-1865—Juvenile fiction.
[1. United States—History—Civil War, 1861-1865—Fiction. 2. Diaries—Fiction.]
I. Garland, Michael, 1952-   ill. II.Title
PZ7.B76625Di 1998
[fic]—dc21   97-22022   CIP   AC
1   3   5   4   2

Author's Note

Not long ago, I saw an exhibit about drummer boys. What a surprise to learn that young drummers led our nation's troops into war until 1864. Brave boys faced battle after battle with nothing but a drum and a pair of sticks.

Two drummer boys especially caught my eye, Orion and Lyston Howe. Both boys were under thirteen years of age when they became drummers. They were too young to go to high school. They couldn't vote. Yet they defended our country in the Civil War (1861-1865). Orion even received our nation's highest military award, the Congressional Medal of Honor.

Orion and his brother withstood many hardships during the war. Some Civil War soldiers kept journals to record their adventures. They described battles, everyday life as a soldier, and the people back home. I never found a journal by Orion or Lyston, but I read old newspapers, books, journals, and letters about the Howes and the war. This book is what I imagine Orion might have written had he kept a journal.

Marlene Targ Brill

$\mathcal{D}$ECEMBER 29, 1860

This journal was Father's idea. He said a man sometimes has thoughts best kept to himself. Since I'm twelve years old today, and almost grown, I should start thinking like a man.

My name is Orion Perseus Howe, and Father is William Harrison Howe. We live on Glen Rock overlooking the bluff above Waukegan Creek in Illinois. Our family moved here two years ago with Cordelia, Father's new wife. We used to live on Auntie and Uncle Shaw's farm. Auntie is Father's older sister. Father worried we were more than Auntie could handle, with her own kids and all. He says Cordelia mothers us now. I told Father I was big enough to take care of Lyston and myself just fine without a mother. I guess this was one of those thoughts Father meant was for writing, not saying.

Lyston was born when I was only twenty months old. Two years later our mother, Eliza Westland Howe, died, and that's when father moved us from Ohio to Auntie Shaw's. I still remember Mother's smile. That's why I can't call Cordelia "Mother."

Then there's Edith. Cordelia and Father say she is our bundle of joy. I say she's a pack of trouble. Just the other day she got hold of some sticks and started poking my drum. She almost ripped the skins off. I grabbed those sticks just in time.

That's what I like best—drumming. Father gave Lyston and me each a drum last year. He taught us to play taps, reveille, sick call, and fall in, fall out. He tells us to beat strong and sure, as the message needs to travel. Cordelia joked that our drumming kept her friends from visiting.

Lyston and I play pretty good. We perform for church picnics and town meetings, sometimes for money. Father played a fife in the Mexican War. Auntie says our fine playing comes from him.

I could drum all day, but Cordelia has different ideas. She has me busier than a cockroach in a flour barrel. I chop wood, haul water, and feed the horses. Sometimes I collect wild dandelions and peppermint or help Cordelia plant wormwood and other roots for when we're sick. I even watch our bundle of *something* if I have to. When Cordelia's through with me, I cut parts for the cabinets Father builds for town folks.

I won't be doing all that for long. Father says if I'm a man, I need to write and do sums like one. He's sending me away to school after the winter wheat is in and the oats and corn planted. Father told me he has big plans for my learning. He gave me this journal as a beginning.

$\mathcal{J}$ANUARY 4, 1861

The Shaws—Auntie, Uncle Samuel, Cousin James, and little Sarah and Nathaniel—came to stay. Uncle Samuel and Father fussed all evening about the farmers down south. It seems many own dark-skinned slaves.

Father says no one has the right to own or sell anyone. Uncle says that people in the South don't want people like Father telling them what to do. These folks really got rattled after Abraham Lincoln won as president fair and square. Because a Southerner didn't win, South Carolina decided not to be part of our Union, the United States. More states threaten to up and leave, too.

I asked if states can just go like that. Father said no. States can't leave whenever things don't go their way. He pounded his fist and called people in those states rebels. He almost broke the table. Then he said he hoped President Lincoln finds a way to bring the rebels back. Cordelia fears a war.

I read about slaves in *Uncle Tom's Cabin*. The book tells how Southern farmers whip their slaves pretty bad. Slave owners even sell children away from their parents. I couldn't think of someone selling me away from Father and Lyston.

$\mathcal{J}$ANUARY 5, 1861

A deep pile of snow fell in the night. After feeding the horses and cows, Cousin James, Lyston, and I built a snow fort near the ravine. James pretended that he was one of those rebels. Lyston was the slave. I pretended to be Henry Blodgett, the man in town who helps runaway slaves escape to Canada. I stole Lyston from James and hid him behind the big red oak. Our hideaway was part of the secret Underground Railroad path.

Then I packed the slave off to the hole in the hickory trunk. After a few great battles in the snow, we all decided Lyston would make it to freedom in Canada. Lyston and I were sorry when James, Auntie, Uncle, and the babies left.

March 22, 1861

All anyone talks about are those fool rebels. I like to slip down to the pier off Water Street and listen to the boat captains. Everybody's arguing about what Lincoln should do now. Most townspeople are against owning slaves. But traders from other parts come with their own ideas about slavery. Folks get pretty worked up when they talk to strangers who don't agree. Last week a man got his face slapped good and hard. Father scolded me for going down to the piers. He doesn't want me where people fight.

March 26, 1861

I planned to sneak down to the piers after chores. Cordelia caught me first. She asked me to watch the baby so she could put her mind to cooking lye. Cordelia likes to boil her lye just right for soapmaking. I hope the butcher wagon comes around while Cordelia's busy. I have some live meat to sell him—Edith!

April 16, 1861

Father sure seemed troubled. He sat quiet through the evening meal, picking at his favorite boiled beef and cabbage. Edith jabbered away, but Father never turned his head.

They're talking about war, he said finally. Southern states are dropping out of the Union like hotcakes. Those rebels fired on Fort Sumter and kicked out our Union soldiers. The worst insult was their tearing down the United States flag. President Lincoln asked each state to send volunteers to defend the Union and the stars and stripes. There's a war meeting tonight at the Opera House.

Father had his fife in his back pocket when he left for the meeting. The candles burned down, and he isn't home yet. Cordelia is downstairs crying. Lyston and I don't know what to think.

April 18, 1861

Tonight Father took Lyston and me to North School to drum at a war meeting. Flags and banners hung around the room like a Fourth of July party. James Wiseman gave a spirited talk about standing by our president no matter what happens. Mr. Sherman told how we'll put down those rebels and be home by summer. Afterward Father, Lyston, and I played lively marches. All the talk fired the men up. But it seemed to me that the music is what pushed the men to sign up to fight. I was getting pretty excited myself!

April 21, 1861

Father, Lyston, and I will play at rallies until our town finds one hundred men for a fighting company. Drumming sure draws a crowd. Then Mr. Wiseman stirs up the men, saying the president needs them.

I said I wanted to enlist, though boys must be eighteen. Mr. Wiseman only laughed at me and said he wanted men, not boys, for this job. I'll show him I can work like any man.

April 25, 1861

I'm truly tired from drumming at nightly war meetings. But it's a good feeling to do something to help. The first Waukegan company just left for Chicago. They drill at Fort Douglas, which is named for Senator Stephen Douglas.

Some two thousand people crowded the train depot to see the men off. Bells rang. People cheered and waved white handkerchiefs. Even little Edith flapped a U.S. flag with one star for each of the thirty-four states, the number before the war. Lyston, Father, and I kept the music coming until the train was long out of sight.

May 15, 1861

President Lincoln called for another 42,000 men. Father has Lyston and me drumming all over Lake County to fill another company. Father asks a lot of questions about Fort Douglas and whispers a bunch to Cordelia. He's talking like he has war fever. So do Lyston and I!

June 5, 1861

Father and Lyston enlisted—without me! Father said Lyston can sign up if he just drums. Father also said that as his oldest son nothing must stop my schooling. Cordelia is to pack me off to Waukegan Academy for the August term. Meanwhile, Lyston, who is only ten years, nine months, and five days, returns to Freeport with Father. They both muster into Company I of the 15th Illinois Regiment. I may never write in this journal again!

July 5, 1861

We finally got a letter today. Lyston wrote that his army drum drags on the ground, him being only four feet two inches. And that's with the strap shortened to the last hole! I wonder how a soldier's drum would fit me.

July 25, 1861

Cordelia and I fear for Father and Lyston. The newspapers are full of Union troubles after Virginia's Battle at Bull Run. I heard down by the pier how our soldiers skedaddled like rabbits at the sight of so many wild-eyed rebs. No one is talking about an easy victory for the North now. The South means to fight and fight hard.

July 26, 1861

Last night I went with Cordelia and Edith to a donation at the courthouse. We helped collect $200 for families in need from the war. Cordelia brought one of her mouthwatering gooseberry pies. I missed Lyston. Uncle Samuel enlisted, and I leave for school next week. At least, no babies wail and whine there.

August 15, 1861

Headmistress Weed is in charge of fifty-four scholars. She tells us she's not afraid to use the rod if we misbehave. We learn arithmetic, writing, spelling, grammar, and science. Tonight I wrote a public-spirited speech to give tomorrow.

Most older boys are gone to war. I practice drums with other fife and drummers during the noon break. We want to be ready when our turn comes to see the elephant. That's what the boys say for leaving home. It's hard to think about lessons with a war going on.

November 4, 1861

Cordelia wrote that Lyston is sick. The surgeon at Camp Hunter in Missouri sent him home with measles, afraid he would die. He better grow fit soon, or I return home.

November 15, 1861

I am pleased Lyston is strong again. Cordelia writes that he ran off to Chicago to drum for those big-city soldiers. I can't stay here like a girl and miss all the excitement. Soldiering must be the best life!

November 22, 1861

I sneaked away from school and returned to Glen Rock. After much pleading, Cordelia agreed to sign for me to enlist. I am most grateful. I can hitch a ride to Chicago with a new company tomorrow. Lyston wrote that he is at Camp Douglas with the 55th Regiment. A regiment is big—ten companies of one hundred men each. Somehow, I will find Lyston.

Cordelia looks tired. She works hard keeping the farm going. She hired some hands to help husk corn. At night she knits socks for soldiers at war and writes Father and Lyston. She has little Edith, too. Right now, Cordelia's fixing some biscuits, bacon, and apples for my train ride. I never thought I'd be sad to leave her.

November 23, 1861

Cordelia and Edith saw me off at the train. Cordelia gave me a pocket-size journal so I can keep writing as Father wishes. She told me to remember my lessons and stay away from shooting rebels. Her talk and Edith's fussing made my stomach knot. I was really going to war now.

November 24, 1861

The men on the train boost my spirits. Many boast about setting those Southerners straight. They sing "The Battle Cry of Freedom" and "The Battle Hymn of the Republic." I get the shivers listening to these grand songs. I can almost smell gunpowder from the South.

November 26, 1861

I hitched a ride from the station to Camp Douglas on a supply wagon. Chicago's as busy as Waukegan. The wagon whizzed past a whirl of people, dusty wooden streets, and tall white houses and stores. My stomach got to talking along the way, so I gobbled what was left of the meal Cordelia had packed.

Camp Douglas was just outside the city. It sat on low sandy hills spotted with black oak bushes. A high fence circled rows of rough wooden buildings that overlooked the same lake that runs past Waukegan. Camp Douglas looked huge, jumping with men learning to be soldiers.

Luckily, Peter Fisher from Waukegan saw me and said he knew where Lyston drilled with Company B. I followed Peter to a building marked "Quartermaster," where men were in line getting clothes and supplies. Then he left me to hunt for Lyston on my own.

All around, men and boys were trying to march in rows. A few in farm clothes stood aside from the others, barking orders. I figure they are officers too new for uniforms. Their hollering "Left, left, left, right, left!" still rings in my ears.

Finally I spotted Lyston and his droopy drum. He seemed pleased to see me, as I was him. He sure knows his way around camp. He found me a place to sleep, which I sorely needed.

NOVEMBER 29, 1861

Lyston plays with the fife and drum corps of the 55th Regiment. Drummers and the regiment brass band bunk together near the officers' quarters. That way players are in earshot of an officer who wants an order drummed to their company of men. I can drum with Lyston as long as I mind the rules. Meanwhile, I have a bunk over Lyston, a warm woolen blanket, and enough to eat.

DECEMBER 4, 1861

All we do is eat, sleep, and drill, drill, drill. We begin before the other soldiers by drumming a morning wake-up call at sunup. The men scramble into line for roll call, looking none too friendly. They are counted then and at evening dress parade. So far, none of us has uniforms or firearms, and all anyone talks about is shooting rebels.

Besides wake-up, we sound lineup, meal calls, and lights out. We're learning other beats that tell foot soldiers to run or stay put. Our rat-a-tats alert other companies how and where we are. We also drum for company drills, some lasting more than seven hours. My shoulders hurt and my feet sting.

At least I'm with Lyston for fife and drum practice. Joe Edwards, Philip Pitts, and I have become chums, too. The older boys call Sylvester Sherman "Betsy." They won't say why. I think it's because he whines like Edith.

December 6, 1861

Food is plentiful. We eat bread, Yankee beans, rice, onions, salted meats, Irish and sweet potatoes, and stewed apples. Sometimes, we have fresh meat or slabs of sowbelly. The only drink is coffee. I guess I better learn to like it.

The real problems are the many cooks who can't cook. Besides measles, fearless men are dying from badly cooked meals. Lyston and I pray for better food at Chaplain Haney's prayer meetings. I miss Cordelia's biscuits and pies.

December 9, 1861

I have never seen such a display. Today we paraded out of Camp Douglas in perfect step. Almost a thousand of us in spit-starched uniforms headed for trains to Camp Benton in St. Louis.

Lyston's drum carried the colors for Company B. When we turned down Chicago's fancy Michigan Avenue, crowds cheered and waved, wanting to give us a merry send-off. The hotel windows were full of people waving white cloths that fluttered like doves. Girls pushed cakes and breads at us. I heard whooping and hollering until we reached the station. I am proud to be almost a soldier.

December 16, 1861

We took two days to reach Camp Benton. Lyston and I chattered about Father and Cordelia's home cooking, getting ourselves a little homesick and hungry at the same time. Then we boarded the steamer *David Tatum* and crossed the great Mississippi River. We tramped five miles to camp in the dark. Night had long been upon us when we arrived. I fell into a bunk in full dress.

A bugle call jolted me awake the next morning. Daylight showed what my sore, chilled body already felt. Only a few straw sticks lined my rough wood bunk, and one blanket too thin to keep out a summer night covered me. The long room has a single large stove to warm our whole company and no window boards to seal out the cold.

Outside, our sleeping quarters face a huge open square. Here we march and parade sunup to sundown. Often the weather quickly shifts from clear and cold to rain. The parade ground turns into a sea of gray mush. On gloomy rainy days us boys try to make our own sunshine. We shed our shoes and socks, roll up our britches, and hop lively through the puddles. Lyston, Joe, "Betsy," Phillip, and I slop along singing "John Brown's Body."

DECEMBER 21, 1861

Everyone drew a pile of new clothing, myself included. Quartermaster Janes handed me a pair of light-blue pants and overcoat, dark-blue jacket, big, heavy shoes, woolen socks and shirt, and a French-style cap that looked like Edith sat on it. He also gave me a rubber blanket, knapsack, canteen, and tin cup for holding food and coffee on the road.

Janes must have thought we were a company of giants. Not much fit, me being only four feet eleven inches. Lyston and I traded clothes around until we found closer-fitting sizes. We still have to roll the sleeves and pant legs.

DECEMBER 29, 1861

Father appeared today! I was well pleased to see him. He transferred into the 55th Regiment to be with Lyston and me. Now he's the regiment's principal musician in charge of us drummers. Somehow I feel surer with him here.

JANUARY 4, 1862

I could shoot more rebels with drumsticks than with our new guns. They are poorly made. They kick like the backside of a mule, too, which almost caused a riot at target practice. Some parts exploded upon firing. They are a danger to the shooter and anyone nearby. The men just throw them about and refuse orders to take arms at dress parade. Sergeant Kendrick wrote Governor Yates and declared we will surrender rather than fight with such worthless popguns.

January 12, 1862

At last we leave tomorrow for the battlefront. Father guesses our steamer, *D. A. January,* will head down the Mississippi River to Cairo, Illinois. He warned us to keep our knapsacks light, as we carry our drums, too. Quartermaster Janes gave me three days' rations, enough food and water for the journey. I can't wait to leave and find me some rebs to whip.

January 21, 1862

Our three-day trip has turned into eight days of hardships. Most of this trip I am tired, hungry, and frozen. The river is a mass of floating ice, and our boat sticks on sandbar after sandbar. My arms ache from hauling supplies off to lighten the load and free the boat, and then hauling them back on again.

Father thought our playing merry tunes would pass the time, but our music does little to quiet the men. Many warm themselves with spirits, becoming drunk and cross. A driving rain and then a snowstorm have made things worse. My only bedding is a blanket and my overcoat. Father caught a deep cough.

January 24, 1862

We finally reached Cairo. The men drained the city of all the food they found. Some paid, and some just didn't. Company B butchered a few hogs and cows. Then our steamer floated up the Ohio River for Paducah, Kentucky. We landed in sunshine and played "Yankee Doodle" in an oak grove.

February 3, 1862

My first real taste of soldiering in the South is no fun. We've tramped for miles through mud and over pitted roads. No one says what we're doing here. My neck hurts from the drum's wide strap. Boys throw away books and keepsakes just to lighten their knapsacks.

Twelve of us sleep like pickles in a barrel under a large cone-shaped tent. The first rainy night, I woke up soaked clear to my skin. Rainwater had run under my bedding. I thought I'd never dry out. Now we dig a ditch around the tent to catch the water.

Father keeps us music makers apart from regular soldiers. We never stand guard or picket duty with the others. Still, we carry water and gather firewood, feed and rub down horses, unload supply wagons, and drum when an officer fancies a tune. By day's end, I am too tired to eat.

FEBRUARY 5, 1862

The 55th seems stuck in this camp at the mouth of the Cumberland and Tennessee rivers. Rumors fly through the regiment about attacking rebels. Other Northern troops send scouts into Kentucky to face the enemy. But never our regiment. Father thinks we are left behind because of our poor guns.

FEBRUARY 6, 1862

Things look brighter. We heard the rebels gave up Fort Henry without a fight. This was their main stronghold on the Tennessee River. And our regiment was issued new guns. They are heavy .58 caliber rifles, which are long and hit the mark. I learned to load and fired some shots. I am pleased with my speed. I plan to shoot me some rebels.

FEBRUARY 10, 1862

Weather has been bitter. Rain, sleet, and snow cloud our daily drills. We slip and slide through the brush outside our camp.

Men keep getting fevers from the cold or sore bellies from spoiled food. Each tent only has one mess pan. The rice is mush, and beans boil up slimy. Lots of us are doing a dance into the woods on account of loose bowels. Father says Joe and I flip the regiment's only good flapjacks. We mix flour, water, grease, and salt, and fry it up.

*F*EBRUARY 15, 1862

Father shoulders many jokes on account of us drummers, especially since the much-loved brass band mustered out. The men call Father "Waukegan" after our hometown. They bellyache that we're troublesome rattlers who jar the nerves. Lyston and I suspect this is in good fun, only I hate being called "runt of the litter." Oftentimes, someone yells "infant drummer" or "half-pint" or pats me on the head like a puppy.

*F*EBRUARY 18, 1862

Our bluecoats captured Tennessee's Fort Donelson on the Cumberland River. Lyston, Joe, "Betsy," and I played "When Johnny Comes Marching Home" while the men tossed their hats in the air.

Then large numbers of wounded from both sides poured into Paducah. Father sent Lyston and me to a church made into a hospital. At first, my legs wobbled at the sight of all that blood, but I never let on. As long as I didn't look too careful, my stomach stayed down. General John Logan of the 31st was foremost in the minds of many. One of the wounded told how Logan mustered his men to fight, even while he was bleeding from two musket balls and had his horse shot out from under him.

*F*EBRUARY 28, 1862

The only time men are quiet is after the mail wagon arrives. Today I received a letter from Cordelia, who worries about us. She read that another battle killed a good many officers. She and Edith get along fine on Father and Lyston's pay and money from the old hog she sold. She got $12.36 for the 412-pounder at 3 cents a pound. But money is tight for some neighbors. Girls have left school to sew for pay. Even the Waukegan *Gazette* now takes yarn or onions, turnips, butter, or chickens for the price of a newspaper.

MARCH 10, 1862

We received urgent orders to strike tents and pack our knapsacks. The 55th scurried about, loading 26 six-mule teams. Our marching music was spoiled by the braying from 156 cranky mules. I think the noise made the men move faster. When everyone was on board, the steamer *Hannibal* headed up the Tennessee River. We're bound for the heart of rebel country to show those Southerners who's right.

MARCH 16, 1862

We docked at Pittsburgh Landing the afternoon of March 11. For three days we played marches for drills, cleaned the steamboat, and took wagons into the countryside to hunt for food. We found a few farms with men gone to war. The women seemed none too pleased to see us but held their tongues. Slaves of all shades and ages gave us corn and fruit saying "Praise the Lord" upon meeting us. One or two followed us back to camp, jumping in with cooking and cleaning and caring for horses. I couldn't help but notice how some had thick scars from whippings. How could a man treat another like that?

On March 14 we joined General Sherman's fleet of eleven regiments, nineteen steamboats, and one gunboat. We headed up the Tennessee to destroy railroads near the river and cut off rebel supplies. A driving rainstorm filled the river, forcing us back. Here we sit at Pittsburgh Landing again, soggy up to our knees in yellow Tennessee mud. Not a man or boy cares to hear our music.

MARCH 25, 1862

Seasons change earlier in Mississippi than Illinois. We camped in a sweet-smelling peach orchard where redbirds sing at sunup. Pink flowers from the trees remind me of spring in Waukegan.

The 54th Regiment Ohio is to our right, among budding oak bushes. Sherman's other regiments pitched tents in a line along ravines, brooks, and rugged bluffs from Locust Creek to Lick Creek. I'd sure like to catch a look at Sherman and General Grant before I head home.

We hear that about 60,000 rebels are fifteen miles down the road in Corinth. I'm ready for some fighting. All we do is tramp ten, twenty miles a day through muddy creeks, dripping trees, and puddled roads. I'll think more fondly of dumb beasts of burden after this war.

APRIL 2, 1862

Phillip and "Betsy" sneak about the woods after dress parade. They return with rabbits, squirrels, and hazelnuts to eat, and straw for bedding. Lyston and I just stew under Father's watchful eye.

APRIL 4, 1862

Rebel guns are firing closer to camp. Last night, I heard pops coming from the Shiloh log church. Drummers up and down the army's front line beat long rolls to signal danger. The men grabbed and loaded their rifles, preparing for a line of fire. Father soon heard that a small clash on the church road ended quickly.

APRIL 8, 1862

I took part in my first great battle, lasting two days on April 6 and 7. Rebels surprised us on the Sabbath as we were shining shoes and cleaning guns for dress parade. A mass of gray and brown swept down from the woods with wild fury. Cannons thundered at our regiment's front.

I swallowed hard and sounded the long roll of danger for Company C. The same alarm pounded down the front, company to company.

Mobs of the enemy turned right toward us. Musket balls crashed around me. Bullets whizzed by my head like a swarm of bees. My heart thumped nearly out of my chest. William Reiman of Company B was first to drop from rapid fire. My stomach tightened. Minutes before he was full of life. Then—still as stone.

I spent the next two days dodging bullets, trying to reach shot-up bodies. We brought water to the wounded and food to fighters. Chaplain Haney, Joe, and I carried every manner of hurt soldier back to the wagons on litters. We drove wagons full of dead and wounded men to a makeshift hospital by the landing.

The end of the first day looked a horror. Dead horses, blood-stained mud, and twisted forms covered the battlefield. The smell of death was everywhere. I offered men spirits to ease their pain. Joe and I held down those needing a limb sawed off, and then we'd just toss the arm or leg on a pile outside.

Ulysses Grant came to check on supplies with Dr. Roler. He looked scruffier and shorter than I expected of a grand general. He went through the hospital right quick chewing on his cigar, and you could see he had some fierce feelings. He was blinking hard as he left. That surprised me.

Joe had an awful fright. In the night, he needed to rest and lay outside the Shiloh log building. Other litter bearers needed to make room inside for more wounded. They tossed the dead in long rows on the ground near the church. Joe awoke in a pile of stinking stiff bodies, he being taken for dead.

The battered rebels finally turned and ran for dear life. We wound up winning the battle. Funny thing is rebels look like our boys except for the uniforms. They die like us, too.

APRIL 10, 1862

It took two days to bury our dead. We dug trenches wide enough to lay a full-grown man crosswise. We carefully placed bodies in rows by company and covered them with Tennessee muck. I carved names I knew on headboards and trees nearby. Then Chaplain Haney led prayers, and we played "Taps" slower than usual. The 55th alone lost more than two hundred lives at Shiloh.

*J*UNE 1, 1862

We planted our flag in the rebel city of Corinth, but there was nobody there to see it. The city was deserted, and when the rebels left they destroyed whatever they couldn't carry.

We returned to camp empty-handed. Food is getting low. I had hardtack and raw meat for breakfast. I haven't had a good scrubbing since Shiloh. My woolen uniform itches something awful under the baking sun.

*J*UNE 26, 1862

We march to and fro at our officers' fancy. Water and rations are scarce. Every few days we fold our tents, load wagons, and tramp through more clouds of dust. For more than a week we've slept under the stars on the lumpy, hard ground. Men are dropping from sunstroke and fever. The dusty, dry air does little to quiet Father's cough.

*J*ULY 31, 1862

About 30,000 of us set up camp at Fort Pickering in Memphis. The 55th Regiment is among large oak trees near the fairgrounds on the road into town. Nearby are large homes with wide porches, fruit orchards, and plenty of springs for water. Father has been very busy with the wagon master, for which I am pleased. I sneak away with chums on field raids for watermelons, peaches, and sweet potatoes. This is the grandest campsite since Chicago.

August 1, 1862

Townspeople are downright nasty about our being here. I guess they heard about Shiloh. Few accept our ideas about keeping the Union together.

Black folks, however, keep trickling into camp, leaving their owners for good. Company C food is a whole lot tastier since some of our black friends arrived. They sure have scary stories to tell, though. Shame on those rebels.

SEPTEMBER 27, 1862

The 55th is part of General Sherman's first brigade now.

Some think Sherman's crazy. Joe and I think most highly of him. Since Shiloh, we call him "Uncle Billy." He's one of us. I spotted him bathing in the river wearing just his scruffy red beard. Some evenings, he joins our campfire after rounds.

OCTOBER 31, 1862

I mustered in today. I repeated an oath and signed my name. The paymaster said he would put in for my thirteen-dollars-a-month pay. I am a proper drummer for Company C of the 55th. I feel like I grew an inch taller today.

NOVEMBER 18, 1862

Letters from home sure brighten a gray day. Cordelia just wrote how she packed eggs in lime and salt for the winter and hung fruits to dry in the cellar. Most crops are in and stored. The rest she sold to the grocer, who still rides by in his wagon. Edith is jabbering up a storm. Cordelia tried to sound cheerful, although she wondered if Father has seen the paymaster lately.

Father has had harsh words with some Chicago soldiers. It seems they don't agree with President Lincoln's new law making slaves free. They worry about soldiering next to black folks. Father said that's a good thing. The war will end sooner. Makes sense to me.

JANUARY 25, 1863

This army sets me to wondering. The rumor going around is we're to capture Vicksburg and clear the Mississippi River of rebels. That way, we cut off boats and trains sending supplies into the heart of rebel country.

Yet we follow the most roundabout path. We've come and gone twice from our snug Memphis camp. We've been up and down the Yazoo River past Vicksburg bluffs. We dig trenches and fire at scattered rebel pickets. Each day we seem farther from whipping those rebels.

Then some 25,000 of us steam upriver to the rebel fort, Arkansas Post. We land, expecting as cruel a fight as at Shiloh. I brace myself for the horrors of gathering the wounded. That night ten-inch shells explode upon our camp, killing three of the 55th and wounding fourteen. Yet by the following afternoon those gutless rebels surrender without another shot.

*F*EBRUARY 9, 1863

Father is lucky to be leaving this swamp. The problem is his lungs are infected again. Dr. Roler ordered him to muster out at once. I'll miss his good judgment during this crazy war. I pray for his safe trip home, his health—and ours. Men are dying of smallpox and malaria in this damp, chilly place. I'm weary of digging and restless to fight.

*F*EBRUARY 15, 1863

I'm homesick. My friend Philip Pitts died of smallpox yesterday. Few letters get through from Cordelia. Father's gone, and I see little of Lyston and Joe. Peter, who is from home, isn't any less gloomy.

Nights can be hardest. Jokes around the campfire about moldy air turn to dreaming aloud about fried ham and biscuits with honey. A few sad sacks sing "Tenting Tonight." Then I have to go sit under a tree. Lately, the words "Thinking of days gone by, of the loved ones at home" make my eyes wet. I'm on my own.

April 23, 1863

Last week our gunboats suffered another failed run to open the blocked river. We've moved camp to drier, higher ground. Weather is warming, so Colonel Malmborg ordered dress parades and drills. Spade and axe are out again, too. Instead of canals, we dig useless roads and build bridges as busywork. Mosquitoes, poisonous snakes, fog, and mold trail us everywhere. I am turning into a frog in all this dampness.

May 9, 1863

We tramp about fifteen miles a day. The heat is blistering. I keep wet hickory leaves in my hat to cool my head. We march down the west side of the Mississippi River, where the grandest plantations stand. Rows of whitewashed slave cabins stretch behind wide mansions facing the road. Modern cotton presses, corn barns, and steam mills hide in back of the slave quarters. Only the people are gone. I guess they fled to Vicksburg for safety. We help ourselves to corn, figs, and other delights from the storehouses.

May 16, 1863

We crossed to the east side of the Mississippi River south of Vicksburg, plodding through deep ravines. My job is to keep the supply wagon wheels from tangling in the thick vines. Food is scarce these days. I live on wormy hardtack and coffee made from swamp water. We're to close in on Vicksburg from the west and north. The distant roar of rebel cannons and rattling muskets warns us of bloody battles ahead.

MAY 27, 1863

This is the first day my head is clear. I have been mending in a field hospital near Vicksburg since May 19. On that fearful day I was wounded in our attack on the last rebel stronghold before Vicksburg's bluffs.

What happened was, we drummed the order down the line to strike at about two o'clock. Three cannonball blasts followed, signaling a mad charge of howling men toward the rebels. I was supposed to return to the rear supply wagons with the other musicians. But I followed our colors to Fort Hill Ditch instead. I joined this war to help, not sit back and watch.

Our main line stopped suddenly where the ditch proved too deep to cross. Heavy fire reached within fifty paces of us, coming from rebels guarding Graveyard Road, which leads to Vicksburg. Our only cover was to lie flat behind the ditch. The zip, zip from pistols made my skin creep. Hamer, Babcock, and Ainsbury of Company C fell dead from head wounds. They were each picked off, one after another, by the same marksman.

Union soldiers loaded and fired one round after another. Then the men started running out of cartridges. Yet rebel fire grew hotter, killing and wounding more men around me.

I took it upon myself to collect cartridges from the bodies. I got across the ditch and up the opposite steep ridge. I filled my shirttails with all I could carry. Then I brought my tiny load to the sharpshooters. Sometimes, I tripped over bodies or tree stumps. I remember hearing a chorus of gasps after one fall, perhaps from men fearing for my safety.

On one trip back, Colonel Malmborg ordered me to the rear wagons for more cartridges. "Bring caliber fifty-four," he yelled after me. The men's muskets were filling with dirt. He thought smaller cartridges would load easier.

I started back, but my path was cut off by rebel fire. I raced toward a clearing. Thick puffs of dust rose where musket balls hit the dry hills. Enemy fire whizzed and zinged past my head. Suddenly, a bullet struck my right thigh. Blood sloshed in my boot like a puddle of water.

I kept climbing the hill but had to stop every few feet. I grew dizzy from loss of blood. My legs wobbled, and my eyes blurred. I worried I couldn't make it to the rear regiment. I think I started to cry.

Somehow I reached the hilltop and level ground. A few yards away, who should I spot but General Sherman, watching the lines. I hobbled to him and cried something like: "General Sherman, please send ammunition to Colonel Malmborg. The men are all out. I can't collect any again."

General Sherman asked my regiment and where the enemy was. He mainly seemed troubled by my bleeding. "Never mind me, send ammunition," I told him. He said he would. As I limped off to the hospital, I remembered the rest of the colonel's message. I turned around and called "Caliber fifty-four."

I hear General Sherman was most impressed that I recalled the cartridge size while so weak. He plans to write Secretary of War Stanton on my behalf.

*J*UNE 28, 1863

The field doctor said the best medicine is home cooking, so I said good-bye to Lyston and struck a beeline for Glen Rock. I hitched a ride on a prisoner boat bound for Cairo. From there a train took me to Chicago. Soon I was on the Chicago & Milwaukee Railroad headed for Waukegan. It's been almost two years since I've been home.

I telegraphed Father about my coming. When the train jarred to a stop, I grabbed my knapsack and hopped and raced as best I could with this shot-up leg.

I flew into Father's wide, strong arms. He told me how proud he was of my soldiering. Then I noticed little Edith looking full grown at almost four years. She greeted me like bright sunshine, jumping about with sparkly-eyed smiles. There's no way I'd sell her to the butcher now.

Teary-eyed, Cordelia hugged me so hard I almost started to bawl myself. I hugged her back. I called her "Mother."

Afterword

General Sherman was true to his word. At Vicksburg, he sent men to lug heavy cartridge boxes to the battlefront. The May 19 attack failed to crack through enemy lines. But the clash proved important to finding out how to break the rebel hold on Vicksburg. The 55th struggled against them on the bluffs until July 4, 1863. Then the rebels surrendered. The Father of Waters, the Mississippi River, was free of rebel blockade.

Over the next few months, Orion's leg healed. As his strength returned, so did his longing to finish the war. On December 25, 1863, Orion reenlisted in the 55th Regiment. This time he was assigned as orderly for General Giles Smith. Orion stayed with the 55th until November 30, 1864, five months before the war ended. By then he had taken part in fourteen battles.

General Sherman barreled east, defeating rebels in his path. Lyston Howe stayed with Sherman's division until he reached the Atlantic. Lyston was the youngest, longest-serving Illinois drummer in the Civil War.

General Sherman wrote a letter to Secretary of State Stanton about Orion, and President Lincoln awarded Orion with entry into the Naval Academy. Years later, after Orion received his schooling as a dentist, the letter reminded others of Orion's courage. On April 3, 1896, he received the Congressional Medal of Honor for bravery under fire at Vicksburg.

Before Vicksburg

MAY 19, 1863

While Sherman stood beneath the hottest fire
That from the lines of Vicksburg gleam'd.
And bomb-shells tumbled in their smoky gyre
And grape shot hiss'd and case shot scream'd.
Back from the front there came,
Weeping, and sorely lame,
The merest child, the youngest face,
Man ever saw in such a fearful place.

Stifling his tears, he limp'd his chief to meet;
But, when he paused and tottering stood,
Around the circle of his little feet
There spread a pool of bright, young blood.
Shocked at his doleful case,
Sherman cried, "Halt! front face!
Who are you? speak, my gallant boy!"
"A drummer, sir, —Fifty-fifth Illinois."

"Are you not hit?" "That's nothing. Only send
Some cartridges. Our men are out,
And the foe press us." "But, my little friend—"
"Don't mind me! Did you hear that shout?
What if our men be driven?
Oh, for the love of Heaven,
Send to my colonel, general dear—"

"I'll see to that," cried Sherman; and a drop
Angels might envy dimm'd his eye,
As the boy, toiling towards the hill's hard top,
Turn'd round, and, with his shrill child's cry
Shouted, "Oh, don't forget!
We'll win yet!
But let our soldiers have some more
More cartridges, sir, caliber fifty-four!"

George Boker, 1864
Atlantic Monthly

Bibliography

Bearss, Edwin, ed. *The 55th Illinois, 1861-1865*. Huntington, WV: Blue Acorn Press, reprinted 1993 (original 1887).

Beyer, W.F., ed. *Deeds of Valor: How American Heroes Won the Medal of Honor*. Detroit, MI: Parrien Kaydel Company, 1905.

Committee of the Regiment. *The Story of the Fifty-fifth Regiment Illinois Volunteer Infantry, 1861-1865*. Huntington, WV: Blue Acorn Press, reprinted 1993 (original 1887).

Crooker, Lucien Bonaparte. "The Drummer Boy of the 55th Ill." SC 358, Folder 2. 1909. Lasalle County School Bulletin.

Dupuy, Trevor. *The Military History of Civil War Land Battles*. New York: Franklin Watts, 1960.

Foner, Eric, and Olivia Mahoney. *The House Divided: America in the Age of Lincoln*. Chicago Historical Society. New York: W. W. Norton & Company, 1990.

Halsey, John, ed. *A History of Lake County, Illinois*. Chicago: Roy Bates, 1912.

Hicken, Victor. *Illinois in the Civil War*. Urbana: University of Illinois Press, 1966.

Johnson, Mark. "Chicago's Civil War." *Eleven* Magazine. September, 1990, pp. 8–11.

Journal of the Illinois State Historical Society, "Chicago's Camp Douglas," LIII, No. 1 (Spring 1960), pp. 41–44.

Keiser, John. *Building for the Centuries: Illinois 1865 to 1898*. Urbana: University of Illinois Press, 1977.

Korn, Jerry. *The Civil War: War on the Mississippi*. Alexandria, VA: Time-Life Books, 1985.

Lawson, Edward. *A History of Warren Township*. Gurnee, IL: Warren-Newport Public Library, 1974.

League of Women Voters. *Waukegan Illinois: Its Past, Its Present*. 3rd edition. Waukegan, IL: City of Waukegan, 1967.

Livermore, Mary. *My Story of the War: A Woman's Narrative of Four Years Personal Experience*. Hartford, CT: A. D. Worthington and Company, 1888.

Mohr, James C., ed. *The Cormany Diaries*. Pittsburgh, PA: University of Pittsburgh Press, 1982.

Murphy, Jim. *The Boys' War*. New York: Clarion Books, 1994.

Nevin, David. *The Civil War: Sherman's March*. Alexandria, VA: Time-Life Books, 1986.

Osling, Louise. *Historical Highlights of the Waukegan Area*. Waukegan, IL: Waukegan Historical Society and City of Waukegan, Bicentennial Commission, 1976.

Sherman, General William T. *The Memoirs of General William T. Sherman, By Himself*. Bloomington, IN: Indiana University Press, 1957.

Snetsinger, Robert, ed. *Kiss Clara for Me*. State College, PA: Carnation Press, 1969.

Stillwell, Leander. *The Story of a Common Soldier*. Alexandria, VA: Time-Life Books, 1983 (originally published Kansas City, MO: Franklin Hudson Publishing, 1920).

Upson, Theodore. *With Sherman to the Sea*. Bloomington, IN: Indiana University Press, 1958.

Walton, Clyde, ed. *Private Smith's Journal*. Chicago: Lakeside Press, 1963.

To Read More About
Drummer Boys and the Civil War

Shorter Books

Kent, Zachary. *The Story of Sherman's March to the Sea*. Chicago: Children's Press, 1987. 48 pages: nonfiction.

Polacco, Patricia. *Pink and Say*. New York: Philomel Books, 1994. 48 pages: fiction.

Longer Books

Collier, James and Christopher. *With Every Drop of Blood*. New York: Delacorte Press, 1992. 235 pages: fiction.

Murphy, Jim. *The Boys' War*. New York: Clarion Books, 1990. 100 pages: nonfiction.